Twenty to Make

Crocheted
Flowers

Jan Ollis

First published in Great Britain 2012

Search Press Limited
Wellwood, North Farm Road,
Tunbridge Wells, Kent TN2 3DR

Reprinted 2012 (twice), 2013

Text copyright © Jan Ollis 2012

Photographs by Debbie Patterson at
Search Press Studios

Photographs and design copyright
© Search Press Ltd 2012

Print ISBN: 978-1-84448-706-6
Epub ISBN: 978-1-78126-040-1
Mobi ISBN: 978-1-78126-095-1
PDF ISBN: 978-1-78126-149-1

Suppliers

If you have difficulty in obtaining any of the
materials and equipment mentioned in this book,
then please visit the Search Press website for
details of suppliers: www.searchpress.com

Printed in Malaysia

Dedication

*I would like to dedicate this book to
my Mother, who taught me to knit,
and my late Great-Aunt Mabel, who
taught me to crochet. Also, to my
partner Ben who has mainly ignored
the various piles of 'work in progress'
stored around our home.*

Terminology and hook sizes

Metric, UK and US crochet hook sizes
are provided in this book. In the patterns
themselves, I have provided both UK and
US crochet terminology – the US term
is given first, followed by the UK term in
brackets. The stitches I have used are:

US terms:	UK terms:
single crochet (sc)	double crochet (dc)
half double crochet (hdc)	half treble crochet (htr)
double crochet (dc)	treble crochet (tr)
treble crochet (tr)	double treble crochet (dtr)
double treble crochet (dtr)	triple treble crochet (ttr)
triple treble crochet (ttr)	quadruple treble crochet (quad tr)

Other terms used:
chain (ch)
space (sp)
slip stitch (ss)
stitch (st); stitches (sts)
slip ring, also known as an adjustable ring

Contents

Introduction

Accessorising can complete an outfit, revitalise a well-loved hat, even add interest to decorations around the home. It is a cheap and relatively quick way of adding those little details that can be expensive to buy on the high street.

I have had great fun designing these twenty crocheted flowers. Most of the patterns need only tiny amounts of materials, making them ideal for using up those half-used balls of yarn, scraps of pretty fabric, beads, buttons and ribbons we all have lying around at home and which 'will come in useful one day'. The yarn I use is mainly no. 3 crochet cotton, which is wonderfully easy to use, though some patterns use other weights of yarn as well as speciality yarns such as fluffy and ribbon yarn. New yarns are being developed all the time and it is exciting to try these out to get different effects.

I have used various crochet hook sizes to make the flowers, and these are given at the start of each project. It is great fun experimenting with different hook sizes and types of yarn; if the flowers turn out slightly different from mine, it doesn't matter at all – it is far better to enjoy the process of making them, and to create something that is unique and personal to you. For this reason, I've given no guidance on tension/gauge, as this will vary depending on the size of hook or type of yarn you use.

Have fun embellishing the flowers as well. Try adding a large, bright button to the centre of the Retro Daisy and stitch it on to a denim jacket or jeans. Make a smaller version of the Camellia, perhaps, and attach it to a hairslide, or make numerous Gazanias in all different colours and sew them on to a plain cushion. I've made all the patterns as easy as possible, so even if you are just learning how to crochet, there will be something in this book for you. Enjoy!

4

The Flowers

Peony, page 8

Pink Cosmos, page 10

Gazania, page 12

Tudor Rose, page 14

Clematis, page 16

Hibiscus, page 18

Foxgloves, page 20

Water Lily, page 22

Poppy, page 24

Freesia, page 26

Daisy Chain, page 28

African Violets, page 30

Camellia, page 32

Passion Flower, page 34

Antique Rose, page 36

Retro Daisy, page 38

Carnation, page 40

Scabious, page 42

Black Orchid, page 44

Orange Blossom, page 46

Peony

Materials and equipment:

Bulky or super bulky yarn in dark red

Double knitting/sport weight yarn in light blue

Crochet hooks, sizes 4.50mm (US G, UK 7) and 2.50mm (US B-1, UK 13)

Bodkin or large-eyed needle for sewing the flower together

Instructions:

With dark red yarn and the larger hook, make 25 ch.

Row 1: miss 1 ch, 2 dc (*UK tr*) into each ch to end.

The work will curl naturally. Form it into 5 rolls, then sew together the ends, making sure the work all faces the same way. Sew together at the centre.

Flower centre

With light blue yarn and the smaller hook, make 5 ch, join with ss into a ring.

*2 ch, 1 dc (*UK tr*), 1 tr (*UK dtr*), 1 dc (*UK tr*), 2 ch, ss, all into centre of loop*, repeat from * to * 4 more times, making 5 petals in total.

Break off yarn, keeping a length of yarn for sewing the flower centre into the middle of the dark red flower.

Add your own distinctive style to a plain hat with this stunning flower.

Pink Cosmos

Materials and equipment:

No. 3 crochet cotton in lime green, pale green and bright pink

Crochet hook size 3.00mm (US D-0, UK 11)

Bodkin or large-eyed needle for sewing in the ends

Instructions:

With lime green crochet cotton, make a slip ring.

Round 1: 2 ch, sc (UK dc) into ring 8 times. Fasten off the lime green crochet cotton.

Change to pale green and ss together.

Round 2: 2 ch, hdc (UK htr) into each sc (UK dc) 8 times, 1 hdc (UK htr) into base ch of 2 ch, join in bright pink and ss into 2 ch.

Make the petal cluster:

2 ch, 1 dc (UK tr), 1 tr (UK dtr), 1 dc (UK tr), 2 ch, ss, all into first ch of 2 ch, hdc (UK htr), sc (UK dc) into next hdc (UK htr), repeat from * to * 8 more times (making 9 petals in total).

Tie off and sew in the ends.

These lovely little flowers work in all sorts of colour combinations. Use them to decorate cushions, lampshades and throws around the home.

Gazania

Materials and equipment:

No. 3 crochet cotton in 3 different colours (A, B and C from the centre outwards)

Crochet hook size 2.50mm (US B-1, UK 13)

Bodkin or large-eyed needle for sewing in the ends

Instructions:

Using colour A, make a slip ring.

Round 1: 1 ch, 10 sc (*UK dc*) into ring. Pull end to close ring.

Fasten off colour A and change to colour B.

ss into first sc (*UK dc*) of ring.

Round 2: 6 ch, ss into base ch, *sc (*UK dc*) into next sc (*UK dc*) of ring, 5 ch, ss into base sc (*UK dc*)*, repeat from * to * 9 times, making 10 petals in total.

Fasten off colour B and change to colour C.

Round 3: insert hook into base ch of first petal.

ss, 7 ch, *ss into base sc (*UK dc*) between petals 1 and 2, 6 ch*, repeat from * to * between each petal base, sc (*UK dc*) 9 times, ss into base of first petal.

Fasten off colour C and sew in the ends.

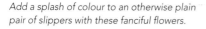

Add a splash of colour to an otherwise plain pair of slippers with these fanciful flowers.

Tudor Rose

Materials and equipment:

No. 3 crochet cotton in white, red and lime green

Crochet hook size 3.00mm (US D-0, UK 11)

Selection of small yellow beads

1 large pearl-shaped bead (pale yellow)

Sewing needle and thread

Bodkin or large-eyed needle for sewing the flower together

Instructions:

For the flower centre, use white crochet cotton and make 4 ch, join with ss into a ring.

3 ch, 3 tr (UK dtr), 3 ch, ss into ring, repeat from * to * 4 more times, making 5 petals in total. Fasten off.

Using red for the back of the flower, make 6 ch, join with ss into a ring.

4 ch, 5 dtr (UK ttr), 4 ch, ss into ring, repeat from * to * 4 more times, making 5 petals in total. Fasten off.

Using green for the leaves, make 8 ch, join with ss into a ring.

7 ch, miss 1 ch, sc (UK dc) into next ch, 2 dc (UK tr), 3 tr (UK dtr), ss into ring, repeat from * to * 3 more times.

7 ch, miss 1 ch, ss into next ch, sc (UK dc) into next ch, 2 dc (UK tr), 2 dtr (UK ttr), ss into base of first leaf. Fasten off.

Lay the red flower on the leaves so that the leaves are visible between each petal. Sew together.

Lay the white flower on the red flower so that the red petals lie between the white petals. Sew together invisibly.

Sew the large pearl-shaped bead into the centre of the white flower, and sew the smaller yellow beads around it.

This gorgeous flower is easy to crochet and will add a unique touch to your home.

14

Clematis

Materials and equipment:

No. 3 crochet cotton in turquoise, pale pink and bright pink

Crochet hook size 3.00mm (US D-0, UK 11)

Bodkin or large-eyed needle for sewing in the ends

Instructions:

Turquoise flower

With turquoise crochet cotton, make 6 ch, ss into loop.

10 ch, ss into loop, repeat from * to * 4 more times, making 5 petals in total.

ss in first 10 ch loop, 2 sc (UK dc), 2 hdc (UK htr), 2 dc (UK tr), 1 hdc (UK htr), 2 sc (UK dc), 1 ss, 2 sc (UK dc), 1 hdc (UK htr), 2 dc (UK tr), 2 hdc (UK htr), 2 sc (UK dc), ss into loop, repeat from * to * into each 6 ch loop.
Fasten off.

Pink flower

Work as for turquoise flower using bright pink crochet cotton. Then:

ss pale pink into first st on outside of a petal, sc (UK dc) into each ch st formed 10 times, 1 ch, ss into same base ch, 10 sc (UK dc) down left-hand side of petal, ss into ring, repeat from * to * around each petal.

Tie off and cut the ends.

What better way to personalise a favourite item than to add a handmade flower in a coordinating colour?

16

Hibiscus

Materials and equipment:

No. 3 crochet cotton in purple and orange

Crochet hook size 3.00mm (US D-0, UK 11)

1 small white bead

15 larger orange beads

Sewing needle and thread

Bodkin or large-eyed needle for sewing the flower together

Instructions:

With purple crochet cotton, make 8 ch, sc (*UK dc*) into 3rd ch, sc (*UK dc*) to end, turn [6 sts].

Row 1: 1 ch, miss 1 ch, sc (*UK dc*) into next 6 ch, turn.

Row 2: 1 ch, sc (*UK dc*) into next 5 sc (*UK dc*), 2 sc (*UK dc*) into last sc (*UK dc*), turn.

Row 3: 1 ch, sc (*UK dc*) into next 6 sc (*UK dc*), 2 sc (*UK dc*) into last sc (*UK dc*), turn.

Row 4: 1 ch, sc (*UK dc*) into next 7 sc (*UK dc*), 2 sc (*UK dc*) into last sc (*UK dc*), turn.

Row 5: 1 ch, sc (*UK dc*) into next 8 sc (*UK dc*), 2 sc (*UK dc*) into last sc (*UK dc*), turn.

Row 6: 1 ch, sc (*UK dc*) into next 9 sc (*UK dc*), 2 sc (*UK dc*) into last sc (*UK dc*), turn.

Row 7: 1 ch, sc (*UK dc*) into next 10 sc (*UK dc*), 2 sc (*UK dc*) into last sc (*UK dc*), turn.

Row 8: 1 ch, miss 1 sc (*UK dc*), sc (*UK dc*) into next 11 sc (*UK dc*), turn.

Rows 9 and 10: repeat row 8 twice.

Row 11: 1 ch, miss 2 sc (*UK dc*), 7 sc (*UK dc*), miss 2 sc (*UK dc*), ss into last sc (*UK dc*).

Row 12: ss, 1 sc (*UK dc*), 2 hdc (*UK htr*) into same sc (*UK dc*), 1 ch, ss into next sc (*UK dc*), ss into next sc (*UK dc*), 1 ch, 2 hdc (*UK htr*) into next sc (*UK dc*), 1 sc (*UK dc*) into next sc (*UK dc*), ss into next sc (*UK dc*).

Fasten off.

Repeat all the above instructions, making 5 petals in total.

For the flower centre, thread the orange beads on to the orange crochet cotton, finishing with the white bead. Make a knot at one end.

Push the white bead up to the knot and ch st around it. Make 1 ch then ch st around an orange bead. Continue to ch st around the beads in the order in which they are threaded. If the flower centre is too loose, wrap the remaining crochet cotton around the beads to make it stable.

Layer the petals so that they overlap slightly leaving a 1cm (½in) hole in the centre. Sew gathering stitches along the bottom edges of all the petals. Draw them together slightly. Place the wider end of the orange-beaded flower centre through this hole and sew it in place securely.

This exotic flower works well in bright, tropical colours. Use it to brighten up your summer clothes, bags and accessories.

Foxgloves

Materials and equipment:

No. 3 crochet cotton in pale pink

Crochet hook size 2.50mm (US B-1, UK 13)

Bodkin or large-eyed needle for sewing in the ends

Instructions:

With pale pink crochet cotton, make a slip ring. 2 ch, 9 sc (*UK dc*), pull together, join with a ss.

Round 1: 2 ch, 9 sc (*UK dc*) into 2nd ch of 2 ch.

Round 2: repeat round 1.

Round 3: 2 ch, 9 hdc (*UK htr*), ss into 2 ch.

Round 4: 3 ch, 9 dc (*UK tr*), ss into 2 ch.

Round 5: 3 ch, 9 dc (*UK tr*), 1 sc (*UK dc*), turn.

Round 6: miss 1 ch, sc (*UK dc*), 2 hdc (*UK htr*) into same dc (*UK tr*), 1 dc (*UK tr*), 1 tr (*UK dtr*), 3 dtr (*UK ttr*) into same dc (*UK tr*), 1 tr (*UK dtr*), 1 dc (*UK tr*), 2 hdc (*UK htr*) into same dc (*UK tr*), 1 sc (*UK dc*), 1 ss.

Tie off and sew in the ends.

These dainty foxgloves look gorgeous adorning tablecloths or napkins.

20

Water Lily

Materials and equipment:

No. 3 crochet cotton in ivory, yellow and green

Crochet hook size 3.00mm (US D-0, UK 11)

Small crystal beads

Sewing needle and cotton thread

Bodkin or large-eyed needle for sewing the
flower together

Instructions:

Take a long length of sewing cotton, fold it in
half and thread the cut ends through the eye
of the sewing needle, forming a large loop.
Thread the crochet cotton into the bodkin
needle and push the bodkin needle and
crochet cotton through the cotton loop. Thread
the beads on to the sewing needle, push them
on to the sewing thread and the crochet thread.
Thread on 42 beads for the centre petals and
72 for the outer petals.

Centre petals (make 6)

Make 7 ch using ivory crochet cotton.

Miss 2 ch, ss, 1 ch, sc (*UK dc*) into next 5 sc (*UK
dc*), ss across base, sc (*UK dc*) into next 5 ch
from other side of ch, ss into top ch, 1 ch, ss
into next sc (*UK dc*), sc (*UK dc*) into next 5 sc
(*UK dc*) to base.

Turn and begin to insert beads. ss into base ch,
*ss with bead into next ch, ss without bead into
next ch*, repeat from * to * twice more, ss with
bead into next ch, ss into top ch, 2 ch, miss 1
ch, ss with bead, *ss with bead into next ch, ss
without bead into next ch*, repeat from * to * 3
more times.

Tie off the end, leave a long length for sewing
in. This makes 1 petal.

Outer petals (make 8)

Make 9 ch with ivory crochet cotton.

Miss 2 ch, ss, 1 ch, sc (*UK dc*) into next 7 sc (*UK
dc*), ss across base, sc (*UK dc*) into next 6 ch
from other side of ch, ss into top ch, 1 ch, ss
into base sc (*UK dc*), sc (*UK dc*) into next 7 sc
(*UK dc*) to base.

Turn and begin to insert beads. *ss into next
ch, ss with bead into next ch*, repeat from * to
* 3 more times, ss with beads into top ch, 3 ch,
miss 2 ch, ss with bead, *ss with bead into next
ch, ss into next ch*, repeat from * to * 3 more
times, ss with bead.

Tie off the end, leave a long length for sewing
in. This makes 1 petal.

Stamen

Wrap yellow crochet cotton around a piece of
card, 5 ch wide, 6 times. Slide the yarn off the
card. Wrap one end of the loops securely and
leave a long length of thread for sewing. Pass
these loops through the hole in the centre of
the flower to the back, secure them, then cut
through the loops on the front of the flower to
make strands.

Leaves

With green crochet cotton, make a slip ring, 2
ch, 6 sc (*UK dc*), pull to join, ss into 2 ch.

Round 1: 2 ch, then 2 dc (*UK tr*) into each sc (*UK
dc*) 6 times, turn.

Round 2: 2 ch, then dc (*UK tr*) into each dc (*UK
tr*), 2 ch into 2 ch sp, turn.

Round 3: sc (*UK dc*) into next dc (*UK tr*), *2 dc
(*UK tr*) into next dc (*UK tr*) three times, 3 dc (*UK
tr*) into next dc (*UK tr*)*, repeat from * to *
5 times, 1 sc (*UK dc*) into next dc (*UK tr*) twice,
1 sc (*UK dc*) into 2 ch sp, ss into next ch,
fasten off.

To make up

Thread the length of yarn attached to one of the centre petals through the bodkin needle, take it across the base of the petal and down on the other side. Pull the yarn so that the petal curls gently inwards. Tie off and cut the thread.

Repeat this with the remaining five centre petals and the eight outer petals.

Take a length of ivory crochet cotton and sew the centre petals together to form a circle, with all the petals facing inwards. Sew the outer petals evenly around the centre petals. Tie off the end securely.

Poppy

Materials and equipment:

Aran/worsted weight yarn in yellow

Double knitting/sport weight yarn in pale blue

Crochet hooks, sizes 3.00mm (US D-0, UK 11) and 3.50mm (US E-00, UK 9)

Toy stuffing

Patterned fabric, 22 x 5cm (8¾ x 2in)

Sewing needle and thread

Bodkin or large-eyed needle for sewing the flower together

Vary the colours and fabric used and create a stunning flower to match your own personal style.

Instructions:

With yellow yarn and a 3.50mm (US E-00, UK 9) crochet hook, make 5 ch.

*Round 1: miss 2 ch, 3 sc (UK dc), turn.

Round 2: 2 ch, dc (UK tr) into base sc (UK dc), dc (UK tr) into next 2 sc (UK dc), dc (UK tr) into last ch twice, turn.

Round 3: 2 ch, dc (UK tr) into base sc (UK dc), dc (UK tr) into next 3 dc (UK tr), 2 dc (UK tr) into last dc (UK tr), turn.

Round 4: 2 ch, dc (UK tr) into base dc (UK tr), dc (UK tr) into next 4 dc (UK tr), 2 dc (UK tr) into last dc (UK tr) sp, turn.

Round 5: miss 1 ch, ss, sc (UK dc), 3 hdc (UK htr), sc (UK dc), ss, turn.

Round 6: miss 1 ch, ss, 3 sc (UK dc), miss 1 ch, ss.

ss 6 sts down top side of petal.*

Do not cut yarn. Repeat from * to *, making 4 more petals.

Cut yarn, leave a long length of yarn for sewing in.

Use the tail of yarn to sew gathering stitches through each of the petals in sequence. Pull them together loosely and join petal 5 to petal 1. Tie and fasten off the yarn.

Tease the top of the petals to curl inwards.

Crochet button

With pale blue yarn and the 3.00mm (US D-0, UK 11) crochet hook, make a slip ring.

Round 1: 1 ch, 10 sc (UK dc) into ring, ss.

Round 2: 1 dc (UK tr) into next sc (UK dc), *2 dc (UK tr) into next sc (UK dc)*, repeat from * to * to end, ss into a ring.

Round 3: *1 dc (UK tr) into next sc (UK dc), miss next sc (UK dc)*, repeat from * to * to end, ss into a ring.

Cut and tie end of yarn, leaving a long length for sewing in.

Stuff with a small amount of toy stuffing.

Sew gathering stitches through the third round, draw up the yarn, sew in the end and fasten off.

Fabric

Fold in each short end of the fabric and press. Fold the fabric lengthways with wrong sides facing. Using sewing thread, sew gathering stitches along the open edge. Pull on the thread and draw the fabric into a circle, leaving a hole in the centre for the crochet button. Sew the sides together securely.

Place the fabric circle in the centre of the crocheted flower and sew them together securely. Stitch the crochet button in the centre of the fabric flower.

Freesia

Materials and equipment:

No. 3 crochet cotton in yellow and green
Crochet hook size 3.00mm (US D-0, UK 11)
Bodkin or large-eyed needle for sewing in the ends

Instructions:

Using green crochet cotton, make a slip ring.

Round 1: 2 ch, sc (*UK dc*) 4 times, join with a ss into 2 ch.

Round 2: 2 ch, hdc (*UK htr*) 5 times into top stitch of sc (*UK dc*), ss into 2 ch.

Round 3: repeat round 2. Change to yellow when ss into 2 ch.

Round 4: 2 ch, *2 hdc (*UK htr*) into next ch,1 hdc (*UK htr*) into next ch*, repeat from * to * twice more, 1 hdc (*UK htr*), ss into 2 ch.

Petal cluster

In the yellow cotton, *3 ch, tr (*UK dtr*), dtr (*UK ttr*), tr (*UK dtr*), 3 ch, ss into base hdc (*UK htr*), ss into next hdc (*UK htr*), ss into next hdc (*UK htr*)*, repeat from * to * 3 more times to make 4 petals.

Tie off and sew in the ends.

Add a touch of springtime to your table with these pretty little freesias.

Daisy Chain

Materials and equipment:

No. 3 crochet cotton in yellow and white
Crochet hook size 2.50mm (US B-1, UK 13)
70cm (27½in) silver-plated cable jewellery chain
100cm (39½in) green sheer organza ribbon
Sewing needle and thread

Instructions:

Single daisy

With yellow crochet cotton, make a slip ring.

Round 1: 1 ch, 8 sc (*UK dc*) into ring, pull end to close ring and remove hook.

Re-insert hook from back of work into first sc (*UK dc*) loop with a ss.

Round 2: change to white crochet cotton, *3 ch, ss into back of each of these 3 ch, ss into next base sc (*UK dc*)*, repeat from * to * 7 times, making 8 petals all together.

ss to centre and tie off the ends.

Double daisy

Follow the instructions for the single daisy up to the end of round 2.

Round 3: work into base ss between petals 1 and 2 of round 2, *sc (*UK dc*), 3 ch, ss into back of each of 3 ch to base ch*, repeat from * to * 7 more times.

sc (*UK dc*) to centre and tie off the ends.

Make seven daisies (some single and some double). Thread the green ribbon through the looped silver necklace and tie it in a knot at the back. Stitch daisies on to the ribbon at regular intervals.

Who could resist this pretty necklace made with hand-crocheted daisies? Alternatively, make them into a stunning hairband or bracelet.

African Violets

Materials and equipment:

No. 3 crochet cotton in violet, yellow and green

Crochet hook size 2.50mm (US B-1, UK 13)

Sewing needle and thread

Bodkin or large-eyed needle for sewing in the ends

Instructions:

With violet crochet cotton, make 4 ch, ss into a circle.

*1 ch, dc (*UK tr*), tr (*UK dtr*), dc (*UK tr*), 1 ch, ss, all into loop*, repeat from * to * 4 more times to make 5 petals.

Tie off the end and press the flower.

Change to yellow crochet cotton and make the central stamen.

3 ch, miss 2 ch, sc (*UK dc*) into ch, ss into base chain.

Tie off the end.

Insert the yellow stamen into the centre of the flower and sew it in place with sewing thread.

Leaf

With green crochet cotton, make a slip ring, 2 ch, 6 sc (*UK dc*), pull to join, ss into 2 ch.

Round 1: 2 ch, then 2 dc (*UK tr*) into each sc (*UK dc*) 6 times, turn.

Round 2: 2 sc (*UK dc*) into each dc (*UK tr*) 12 times, 1 sc (*UK dc*) into 2 ch, 2 dc (*UK tr*) into 2 ch, 1 sc (*UK dc*) into 2 ch, ss into 2 ch.

Fasten off.

Bring a forgotten yet much-loved possession back to life with these brightly coloured flowers.

Camellia

Materials and equipment:

Bulky or super bulky yarn in pink

Crochet hook size 4.50mm (US G, UK 7)

Lightweight fabric, such as lace or voile

Heavyweight fabric, such as a furnishing
cotton linen

Tracing paper

Pencil

Scissors

Assorted beads and vintage buttons

Sewing needle and thread

Instructions:

Make 5 ch, join with ss into a ring.

*2 ch, 1 dc (UK tr), 1 tr (UK dtr), 1 dc (UK tr),
2 ch, ss, all into the centre of the loop*, repeat
from * to * 4 more times to make 5 petals.

Break off the yarn.

Press the crocheted flower gently.

Cut a circle of lightweight fabric the same
diameter as your flower.

Draw around the flower on tracing
paper and cut out a template. Pin the
template on to heavyweight fabric
and cut out a fabric flower.
Set aside.

Attach the lightweight fabric
circle to the crocheted flower,
stitching in a circle 1cm (½in)
from the centre of the flower.

Sew buttons and large beads
in the centre of the flower,
then fill in the gaps with
smaller beads.

Lay the beaded crocheted
flower on to the heavyweight
fabric flower and sew it in place
invisibly from the back.

*This design has a classic vintage
feel. It works well in different colour
combinations and with a variety of
buttons and beads.*

Passion Flower

Materials and equipment:

No. 3 crochet cotton in cream and pale green

Fluffy yarn in blue/black

Double knitting/sport weight yarn in lime green and purple

Crochet hook size 3.00mm (US D-0, UK 11)

Sewing needle and thread

Bodkin or large-eyed needle for sewing the flower together

Instructions:

Petals

Work from the centre of the flower outwards.

Using cream crochet cotton, make a slip ring.

2 ch, 6 sc (*UK dc*) into ring, pull to close, ss into top ch of 2 ch.

Round 1: 1 ch, 1 sc (*UK dc*) into base sc (*UK dc*), 2 sc (*UK dc*) into each of next 7 ch, ss into 1 ch.

Round 2: 1 ch,1 sc (*UK dc*), *2 sc (*UK dc*), 1 sc (*UK dc*), 1 sc (*UK dc*)*, repeat from * to * 4 more times, 1 sc (*UK dc*), ss into 1 ch.

Round 3: 1 ch, *2 sc (*UK dc*) into next sc (*UK dc*), 1 sc (*UK dc*) into next sc (*UK dc*)*, repeat from * to * 9 more times.

Join in the pale green crochet cotton and ss into 1 ch. Fasten off the cream cotton.

Using the pale green cotton, *10 ch, miss 2 ch, dc (*UK tr*) into next 4 ch, hdc (*UK htr*) into next 4 ch, ss into next sc (*UK dc*) of round 4, turn, ss into next 8 ch, sc (*UK dc*) into 2 ch sp, turn, dc (*UK tr*) into next 4 ch, hdc (*UK htr*) into next 4 ch, ss into next sc (*UK dc*) from round 3, ss into next sc (*UK dc*)*, repeat from * to * 9 more times. Fasten off.

Join the fluffy yarn at the base of petal 1, *3 ch, ss into base of next petal*, repeat from * to * 9 more times. Fasten off.

Flower centre

With lime green yarn, 4 ch, ss into ring, sc (*UK dc*) into ring, 4 ch, miss 1 ch, hdc (*UK htr*) into next ch, ss into next ch twice, ss into ring, *3 ch, miss 1 ch, hdc (*UK htr*) into next ch, ss into next ch, ss into ring*, repeat from * to * 3 more times. Fasten off.

With purple yarn, 3 ch, miss 1 ch, 1 hdc (*UK htr*), 1 ss. Place this in the middle of the lime green flower centre and sew it in place securely.

Sew the flower centre to the middle of the passion flower.

This stunning creation looks fabulous on clothes, bags and accessories.

Antique Rose

Materials and equipment:

Double knitting/sport weight yarn in blue

Crochet hook size 3.00mm (US D-0, UK 11)

Lightweight woven fabric, 60cm (23½in) long, tapering
from 3 to 1cm (1¼ to ½in) evenly along one long edge

Sewing needle and thread

Bodkin or large-eyed needle for sewing the flower together

Instructions:

With blue yarn, make 100 ch.

Petals 1–3: miss 2 ch, 1 hdc (*UK htr*) into next
ch, 1 dc (*UK tr*) into next ch, 1 hdc (*UK htr*) and
2 ch into next ch.

*ss into ch, 2 ch and 1 dc (*UK tr*) into next ch,
1 tr (*UK dtr*) into next ch, 1 dc (*UK tr*) and 2 ch
into next ch*, repeat from * to * twice more.

Petals 4–6: *ss into ch, 2 ch and 1 dc (*UK tr*) into
next ch, 1 dc (*UK tr*), 1 tr (*UK dtr*), 1 dc (*UK tr*)
into next ch, 1 dc (*UK tr*) and 2 ch into next ch*,
repeat from * to * twice more.

Petals 7–9: *ss into ch, 3 ch and 1 tr (*UK dtr*)
into next ch, 1 tr (*UK dtr*), 1 dtr (*UK ttr*), 1 tr (*UK
dtr*) into next ch, 1 tr (*UK dtr*) and 3 ch into next
ch*, repeat from * to * twice more.

Petals 10–13: *ss into ch, 3 ch and 1 tr (*UK dtr*)
into next ch, 2 tr (*UK dtr*), 1 dtr (*UK ttr*), 2 tr (*UK
dtr*) into next ch, 1 tr (*UK dtr*) and 3 ch into next
ch*, repeat from * to * 3 more times.

Petal 14: *ss into ch, 3 ch and 1 tr (*UK dtr*) into
same ch, 1 tr (*UK dtr*) into next ch, 2 tr (*UK dtr*)
into next ch, 2 dtr (*UK ttr*) into next ch (twice), 2
tr (*UK dtr*) into next ch, 1 tr (*UK dtr*) into next ch,
1 tr (*UK dtr*) and 3 ch into next ch*, repeat from
* to * 3 more times.

Tie and cut the yarn.

Press the crocheted work and the length of
fabric. Fray the edges of the fabric and lay it on
top of the crochet, right side up. Sew gathering
stitches along the bottom edge starting from
the narrow end and working into the middle.
Draw up the thread loosely, forming the shape
of the flower. Secure the first half of the flower
with a few stitches and repeat the process
starting from the centre and working to the
other end. Tie off the ends.

*This pretty flower has a fresh,
country feel. For a more vintage
look, use peach-coloured
crochet cotton and muted
brown lace.*

Retro Daisy

Materials and equipment:

No. 3 crochet cotton in orange, purple, white, turquoise, yellow and dark green

Crochet hook size 3.00mm (US D-0, UK 11)

Sewing needle and thread

Bodkin or large-eyed needle for sewing in the ends

Instructions:

Orange flower

With orange crochet cotton, 8 ch, ss into ring.

Round 1: 1 ch, 12 sc (*UK dc*), join with ss.

Round 2: 9 ch, ss into base sc (*UK dc*), ss into next ch, ss into next ch, *10 ch, ss into next ch, ss into next ch*, repeat from * to * three more times, 10 ch, ss to next ch (makes 6 petals).

Round 3: *ss into centre of first 10 ch, 20 sc (*UK dc*) along length of ch, ss into base sc (*UK dc*)*, repeat from * to * 5 more times working into the centre of each 10 ch sp.

Cut and tie off the end.

Orange flower centre

Round 1: with purple crochet cotton, make a slip ring, 1 ch, 6 sc (*UK dc*).

Change to white crochet cotton, ss into 1 ch.

Round 2: 1 ch, 2 hdc (*UK htr*) in each sc (*UK dc*), ss into 1 ch.

Cut and tie off the ends.

Stalk

With dark green crochet cotton, make 20 ch, miss 1 ch, sc (*UK dc*) down length of ch, 1 ss across bottom of ch, 20 sc (*UK dc*) to top of ch.

Fasten off and sew in the ends.

Lay the flower centre in the middle of the orange daisy petals, sew them together securely and fasten off.

Turn the flower over, place the stalk so that the top is in the centre of the daisy petals and sew it in place securely with cotton thread.

Turquoise flower

This is made in the same way as the orange flower, but without the flower centre and stalk.

Yellow flower

With yellow crochet cotton, 6 ch, ss into ring.

Round 1: 1 ch, 10 sc (*UK dc*), join with ss.

Round 2: 7 ch, ss into base sc (*UK dc*), ss into next ch, ss into next ch, *8 ch, ss into next ch, ss into next ch*, repeat from * to * twice more, 8 ch, ss to next ch (makes 6 petals).

Round 3: *ss into centre of first 8 ch, 16 sc (*UK dc*) along length of ch, ss into base sc (*UK dc*)*, repeat from * to * 5 more times working into the centre of each 8 ch sp.

Cut and tie off the end.

Add a splash of colour to your summer picnic
or barbeque with these fun flowers.

Carnation

Materials and equipment:

No. 3 crochet cotton in red and pink

Crochet hook size 3.00mm (US D-0, UK 11)

Sewing needle and thread

Bodkin or large-eyed needle for sewing the flower together

Instructions:

With red crochet cotton, make 31 ch.

Row 1: miss 1 ch, 2 dc (*UK tr*) into each ch, 1 ch, turn.

Row 2: 2 hdc (*UK htr*) into each ch, 1 ch, turn. Fasten off the red yarn and join in the pink.

Row 3: *3 ch into next ch, ss into next ch*, repeat from * to * to end of row.

Tie off the end, but leave a good length. Draw this length through the base chain in a loose gathering stitch. Pull up the work, tease the flowers into shape and pull the yarn through the petals to secure.

Small flower

To make a smaller flower you will need no. 1 crochet cotton in red and a size 2.50mm (US B-1, UK 13) crochet hook. Here I have made a pretty ring by attaching the flower to a ring base using fabric glue.

Make 25 ch.

Row 1: miss 2 ch, 2 sc (*UK dc*) into each ch to end, turn.

Row 2: miss ch, 2 sc (*UK dc*) into each sc (*UK dc*) from row 1.

Row 3: miss ch, 2 hdc (*UK htr*) into each sc (*UK dc*) from row 2 to last 10 sc (*UK dc*), 1 sc (*UK dc*) to end, 1 sc (*UK dc*) 3 times in side sts to beginning.

Tie off the end, leaving a length of yarn around 15cm (6in) long. Use the thread to sew loose gathering stitches through the base chain. Pull up the work and form it into a circle. Sew the sides together securely.

For a more subtle effect, the carnation can be worked in a single colour, as shown by the pale green version in the photograph on the right.

Scabious

Materials and equipment:

Multicoloured ribbon yarn

Crochet hook size 4.50mm (US G, UK 7)

9 red bugle beads

9 small red beads

Sewing needle or beading needle and thread

Bodkin or large-eyed needle for sewing the flower together

Instructions:

Make 4 ch, join with a ss into a ring.

Round 1: *ss into loop, 7 ch, miss 2 ch, ss into next 5 ch*, repeat from * to * 10 more times (11 petals).

Round 2: *ss into space between petals 1 and 2 from round 1 keeping yarn behind, 6 ch, miss 2 ch, ss into next 4 ch*, repeat from * to * 10 more times, working between the petals from round 1. You should now have made 11 more petals, making 22 petals in total.

Round 3: *ss into base ch between petals 1 and 2 from round 2, 5 ch, miss 2 ch, ss into next 3 ch*, repeat from * to * 10 more times, working between the petals. You should now have made 11 more petals, making 33 petals in total.

Round 4: ss into base of first petal from round 3, break yarn and thread through to back of work.

Thread a needle with sewing thread and bring the thread through to the centre of the flower from the back. Thread on a bugle bead followed by a small bead, then pass the needle through the bugle bead again. Leave the thread slightly loose so that the beads are not held too tightly. Repeat for the remaining beads then secure on the back of the work with a few stitches.

Attach the flower to a ribbon to make it into a pretty bracelet, as shown in the photograph on the facing page.

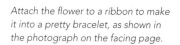

Black Orchid

Materials and equipment:

Black ribbon yarn

Crochet hook size 3.50mm (US E-00, UK 9)

40cm (16in) length of black organza ribbon

27cm (10¾in) length of narrow black satin ribbon

Various small black and clear beads

Sewing needle and thread

Bodkin or large-eyed needle for sewing in the ends

Instructions:

Make 10 ch, ss into a ring.

Round 1: *3 ch, dtr (UK ttr) into ring, ttr (UK quad tr), 3 ch, miss 2 ch, sc (UK dc) into first ch, 2 ttr (UK quad tr), dtr (UK ttr), 3 ch, sc (UK dc) into ring*, repeat from * to * twice more, making 3 petals.

5 sc (UK dc) around the base ring. Press the flower.

Round 2: 2 ch, ss into centre base of petal 1, 4 ch, ss into centre base of petal 2, 4 ch, ss into centre base of petal 3, 2 ch, ss into base sp of petal 3, 5 sc (UK dc) in sc (UK dc) of base ring, 2 sc (UK dc) into 2 ch sp.

sc (UK dc) into 4 ch sp, 3 ch, dtr (UK ttr), ttr (UK quad tr), 3 ch, miss 2 ch, sc (UK dc) into first ch, 2 ttr (UK quad tr), dtr (UK ttr), 3 ch, sc (UK dc) into 2 ch sp, repeat from * to * to end of round.

Five petals have now been made: 3 larger petals at the back of the work and two slightly smaller petals at the front. Do not cut the yarn. Press all the petals.

Who says crochet and glamour don't mix? This stunning black orchid will add a touch of sophistication to any outfit.

Centre front petal (lip)

5 ch, ss into base of petal 4, turn.

Round 3: 2 ch, [hdc (UK htr), 3 dc (UK tr), hdc (UK htr)] into 5 ch sp from round 2, ss into base of petal 5.

Round 4: 4 ch, ss into base of petal 4 (push the lobe upwards to fill the gap made by 10 ch loop), turn.

Round 5: 1 ch, sc (UK dc), hdc (UK htr), 3 dc (UK tr), hdc (UK htr), sc (UK dc), ss into base of petal 5, turn.

Round 6: work into sts from round 5. 1 ch, miss 1 sc (UK dc), 2 hdc (UK htr), dc (UK tr), 3 ch, miss 2 ch, ss into ch, dc (UK tr), 2 hdc (UK htr), sc (UK dc), ss into base of petal 4.

Tie and fasten off the end.

Note: it is important that the lobe created in round 4 is pushed up to fill the gap. It should then be sewn in place before attaching the ribbons and beads (see below).

Cut the organza ribbon into 4 lengths and stitch them into the centre of the flower, above the lip. Cut the satin ribbon into 2 unequal lengths and attach them on top of the organza. Sew a cluster of black and clear beads in the centre of the flower.

Orange Blossom

Materials and equipment:

No. 3 crochet cotton in yellow and white

Crochet hook size 2.50mm (US B-1, UK 13)

Various small orange beads

Sewing needle and orange thread

Bodkin or large-eyed needle for sewing in the ends

Instructions:

Using yellow crochet cotton, make 4 ch, join with a ss into a ring.

Round 1: 1 ch, 5 sc (*UK dc*) into ring, ss into 1 ch.

Round 2: 2 ch, 1 dc (*UK tr*) into each sc (*UK dc*), ss to join, tie off the end.

Rejoin white crochet cotton at base of work, work into sc (*UK dc*) strand.

Round 3: *6 ch, miss 1 ch, 1 sc (*UK dc*) into next ch, 1 hdc (*UK htr*) into next ch, 1 dc (*UK tr*) into next ch, 1 tr (*UK dtr*) into next ch, 1 dtr (*UK ttr*) into next ch, ss into next st of first round*, repeat from * to * 4 more times, making 5 petals in total. End in same st as join.

Tie off and sew in the ends.

Join the sewing thread to the reverse of the flower and push the needle up through the space between the yellow centre and the white ridge surrounding it. Thread on a bead and take the thread back through to the back of the work. Repeat, sewing on beads all around the yellow flower centre.

These pretty little flowers look great on accessories around the home – try them on hanging hearts, napkin rings, jewellery boxes and notebooks, for example, to add that personal touch.

Acknowledgements

Thanks to DMC for donating many of the yarns needed to create the crocheted flowers in this book; Katie Sparkes and Roz Dace at Search Press for their help and assistance; Mandy Wools of Wells, for their expertise; and Sue Kerton for her unending patience. But most importantly, my family and friends for their constant support and encouragement.